Workplace Companion

STUDENT WORK-BASED LEARNING NOTEBOOK

Carl G. Sargent

Prentice
Hall

Upper Saddle River, New Jersey
Columbus, Ohio

Vice President and Publisher: Jeffery W. Johnston
Acquisitions Editor: Sande Johnson
Assistant Editor: Cecilia Johnson
Production Editor: Holcomb Hathaway
Design Coordinator: Diane C. Lorenzo
Cover Designer: Thomas Borah
Cover Art: Julie Delton/Artville
Production Manager: Pamela D. Bennett
Director of Marketing: Kevin Flanagan
Marketing Manager: Christina Quadhamer
Marketing Assistant: Barbara Rosenberg

This book was set in Berkeley Book by Aerocraft Charter Art Service.
It was printed and bound by Banta Book Group.

Prentice-Hall International (UK) Limited, *London*
Prentice-Hall of Australia Pty. Limited, *Sydney*
Prentice-Hall Canada Inc., *Toronto*
Prentice-Hall Hispanoamericana, S.A., *Mexico*
Prentice-Hall of India Private Limited, *New Delhi*
Prentice-Hall of Japan, Inc., *Tokyo*
Pearson Education Singapore Pte. Ltd.
Editora Prentice-Hall do Brasil, Ltda., *Rio de Janeiro*

10 9 8 7 6 5 4 3 2 1
ISBN 0-13-093106-3

Contents

To the Teacher/Coordinator

Welcome to work-based learning. This exciting, inspiring part of education takes students into the community to experience new thoughts and feelings about the world around them. The activities found in this workbook will build on and enrich concepts and skills students have learned in the classroom. The workbook will also facilitate guided learning and portfolio development during service-learning opportunities. As part of this process, students will have the opportunity to build positive work habits and attitudes that will make them outstanding employees.

A STUDENT NOTEBOOK SERVES AS A MULTIPURPOSE TOOL:

- It is an excellent resource and means of data collection for student portfolios.
- It gives students a way to express concerns, thoughts, and feelings about their work.
- It addresses individual career goals.
- It ties classroom instruction and learning to real-world experiences.

KEY COMPONENTS TO REMEMBER:

1. Whenever possible, discuss the purpose of work-based learning and review the notebook contents with each student. Help students to be successful by clarifying expectations and requirements.

2. To ensure success, students should demonstrate appropriate readiness skills before they enter the workplace. To develop readiness skills, students require instruction or experience in work habits, attitudes, and behavior. Readiness skills include but are not limited to the following:

PERSONAL READINESS SKILLS

Communication, both written and oral

Social manners

Business manners

Self-esteem

Knowledge of workplace attire and grooming

Knowledge of workplace ethics

Appreciation for safety, confidentiality, and the potential for harassment

WORK READINESS SKILLS

Resume preparation

Letter of application preparation

Interviewing

Thank-you letter preparation

Understanding American workplace culture

Skills employers want—SCANS skills and competencies

Students can verify or document their readiness skills through class instruction, positive work evaluations, or personal recommendations. Set criteria that you think are reasonable and reachable for students.

3. Be sure to include a review or instruction in the SCANS skills and competencies. Students may need to practice writing and identifying these skills through simulated examples.

4. The Student Information and Review section is for students to use as a reminder of previously learned skills, requirements, and expectations. It will be particularly useful when students match SCANS skills to their job tasks.

5. Give each student an interest inventory to help narrow the options for placement. Students also may want to explore options and search for jobs by computer.

USING THE PROGRAM

The program can be used as an independent study or as part of a class course curriculum. Meet with students individually or as a group to discuss their goals, and how participation fits into their career objective or degree/diploma program. Groups and individuals may greatly vary in their readiness level; therefore, readiness instruction may be required. You may also want to stagger job placements to fit time constraints and available resources.

At the conclusion of the program, arrange for the students to give a formal class presentation about their experience. This exercise will help students internalize their total experience by summarizing and organizing their activities, identifying strengths and weaknesses, and sharing with others.

Consult with your state's Department of Education and ask for its work-based learning manual. This manual will contain all the necessary forms and procedures for establishing community sites, including training agreements, examples of learning objectives, and more. The department will also have information on work-based learning and readiness curricula.

To Students

This notebook is for you. The goal of this work-based learning program is to help you explore and participate in a career activity for which you show interest and aptitude. Your community experience can be a positive and enriching part of your education.

To participate in this type of program, you must bring to it appropriate workplace habits, attitudes, and behavior. Employers are eager to teach you new skills and aspects of their industry. But for a business to accomplish this, you must be cooperative, display a mature attitude, and show social competence. Your teacher or work coordinator will assist you in meeting these objectives.

BE PREPARED TO ANSWER THE FOLLOWING QUESTIONS REGARDING READINESS:

- Are you a reliable and punctual person?
- Can you follow multiple directions and complete tasks promptly?
- Are you willing to conform to the dress code of the business in which you are placed?
- Are you well groomed and polite, and do you display a positive attitude?
- Are you a good listener and able to communicate your ideas in a clear and concise manner?
- Do you get along well with adults?
- Are you eager to learn and receptive to constructive criticism?
- Do you have a professional resume?

If your answers to these questions are yes, you may have the necessary readiness skills to get started.

Once you have demonstrated that you are competent in readiness skills, your school contact and business representative can help you develop a work-based learning plan. You are expected to make an honest attempt at reaching your goals during the course of the experience. Even though plans and work designs may change, you are expected to adapt to these changes and participate in appropriate responses.

As part of the plan, you will identify specific learning objectives, with the help of your business partner and your program coordinator. These objectives are taken directly from the list of necessary skills developed by employers and they will help you focus on the important components of high-quality work.

To make the most of your experience, follow the provisions in the student handbook and complete a work-based learning contract. Enter data regularly and keep up to date on your personal journal. During the experience, you will also choose a project or problem that directly relates to the experience. At the conclusion of the work-based experience, you might be asked to share the results of your activity with the class or teacher by giving a formal presentation.

Enjoy, work hard, and begin the program with confidence. You are about to start a memorable experience that will enhance your future.

Acknowledgments

I would like to thank numerous people for their assistance in putting this notebook together. First, a special thanks to the students who participate in our high school transition program and career classes. Their recommendations and suggestions were extremely relevant and valuable. I also appreciate the reviewer input from several school-to-career coordinators and special educators in our region. A personal thanks to my business partners and family, who have always been supportive of innovative projects that help students see the connection between work and school.

About the Author

Carl Sargent, a native of Seattle, has been in education for over 20 years, teaching and counseling students at various stages of their educational and career development. He believes current educational goals and restructuring can be achieved through partnerships between schools and the community. Work-based learning activities are a significant part of this process at all educational levels.

In the last ten years, Sargent has been involved in Oregon's school-to-work efforts as a Transition Services Coordinator, providing work-based learning opportunities to special population students. He is a member of several local community and educational committees.

Sargent has written four books related to including all students in workplace learning programs and connecting activities between business and education. He has been a presenter on special populations and school-to-work issues at local, state, and national conferences.

Student Information and Review

chapter 1

This section helps you review concepts and issues related to community placement in work-based learning. Use these pages as a reference or study guide when filling out your journal, when writing your final presentation or summary, and for reminders during your preparation and training.

WHAT IS WORK-BASED LEARNING?

Work-based learning is learning that takes place in the community, at a local business or agency. Broadly, the term describes a menu of student opportunities to learn about the world of work. These include structured work experiences, internships, mentorships, and community service learning opportunities. Its major purpose is to link school learning to practical, real-life activities outside the school, and to help students begin lifelong career development.

Work-based learning usually takes place once you have participated in career awareness activities and exploration. These may include field trips, listening to classroom speakers, research, career assessments, and general work experiences.

WHY WORK-BASED LEARNING?

Many young students today are not equipped with the academic and work skills they need to qualify for further education and training programs, or to perform jobs in our competitive global economy. Work-based learning addresses the problem by making learning relevant. It creates a combined community and school effort to prepare you for the future. The work-based system is a way for schools to focus teaching and learning on what the communities and businesses are asking for. It transforms workplaces into places of learning, and brings the workplace into the classroom.

BENEFITS OF WORK-BASED LEARNING FOR STUDENTS

Applies classroom learning to real-life situations

Helps you explore career opportunities

Improves work habits and attitudes

Motivates students to stay in school

Establishes a connection between classroom learning and work

Helps you make clear decisions

Provides an educational structure

Helps you identify your own interests, goals, and aptitudes

BENEFITS OF WORK-BASED LEARNING FOR COMMUNITY

Helps create a pool of qualified future workers

Reduces employer training costs

Offers workers a chance to be involved in education

Builds a positive cooperative environment linking work and education

Helps employers and educators share resources

WHAT EMPLOYERS EXPECT FROM STUDENTS

Workplace conditions are continually changing to meet the demands of today's global economy, but the basic skills for success remain the same. Employers have combined their resources to identify fundamental skills that are important for all school- and work-based learning programs. The U.S. Department of Labor presented these findings in a report to the nation in 1991. They are referred to as the SCANS (The Secretary's Commission on Achieving Necessary Skills and Competencies). By mastering these skills you will be in a position to compete for high-paying, skilled professions.

What Are the Essential Skills?

The SCANS skills and competencies are the tools that business and labor are requesting schools teach students. These are specific work habits, attitudes, and performance objectives that will prepare you for the high-skilled, high-performance jobs of the future.

ESSENTIAL SKILLS AND COMPETENCIES (SCANS)

Foundation Skills

BASIC SKILLS

Listening. Receives, attends to, interprets, and responds to verbal directions and cues.

Speaking. Organizes ideas and communicates orally, communicates thoughts well, speaks clearly.

Writing. Communicates thoughts and ideas in writing; creates documents, reports, and charts.

Mathematics. Performs basic computations and practical problems, is accurate, applies skills to job.

Reading. Reads and comprehends instructions, interprets written information.

THINKING SKILLS

Decision making. Considers risks, evaluates and chooses best alternatives, identifies goals.

Problem solving. Recognizes problems and develops or implements plans for action.

Creative thinking. Generates new and innovative ideas.

Knowing how to learn. Uses learning techniques to acquire new knowledge and skills.

Reasoning. Discovers a rule or standard fundamental to the relationship between two or more objects and applies it when problem solving.

(continued)

PERSONAL QUALITIES

Self-esteem. Maintains a positive view of self and believes in own self-worth.

Responsibility. Shows a high level of effort and works toward achieving goals.

Sociability. Demonstrates understanding, adaptability, empathy, politeness, and friendliness.

Integrity/honesty. Shows ethical standards and follows through with courses of action.

Self-management. Assesses self accurately, sets personal goals, monitors own progress, and shows self-control.

Competencies

RESOURCES

Time. Selects activities and goals in an orderly fashion, allocates adequate time, prepares and follows schedules.

Money. Uses and prepares budgets, keeps records, forecasts and makes adjustments.

Material and facilities. Acquires, stores, locates, and uses materials or space efficiently.

Human resources. Assesses skills and distributes work, evaluates performances and gives feedback.

INTERPERSONAL

Participates as team member. Engages and contributes to a group effort.

Teachers others new skills. Demonstrates ability to give direction and show others by example.

Serves clients. Works to satisfy customers to their expectations.

Exercises leadership. Communicates ideas to others, persuades and convinces others, shows responsibility when changing policies or procedures.

Negotiates. Works toward agreements and resolves differences.

Works with diversity. Works well with men, women, and individuals with diverse backgrounds.

INFORMATION

Acquires and evaluates information.   **Interprets and communicates information.**

Organizes and maintains information.   **Uses computers to process information.**

SYSTEMS

Understands systems. Knows how social, organizational, and technological systems work and shows ability to operate them effectively.

Monitors and corrects performance. Distinguishes trends, predicts impact on systems operations, diagnoses performance and malfunctions in systems.

Improves or designs systems. Suggests modifications and develops new or alternative ways to improve performance in systems.

TECHNOLOGY

Selects technology. Chooses appropriate procedures, tools, and equipment.

Applies technology. Understands intent and procedures for operations.

Maintains and troubleshoots equipment. Prevents, identifies, or solves potential problems.

EXAMPLES

The following are examples of typical work experiences and SCANS competencies that relate to specific job tasks. Use this as a guide when completing your journal entries and identifying the correlation between task and competency.

Activity

Take responsibility for keeping work area looking pleasant, neat, and efficient.

FOUNDATION SKILLS

Basic skills: Listening, speaking

Thinking: Decision making, creative thinking, reasoning

Personal qualities: Responsibility, self-management

COMPETENCIES

Interpersonal: Participates as team member, teaches others new skills

Systems: Understands systems

Activity

Conduct an inventory of supplies and notify supervisor of items to be replaced or ordered.

FOUNDATION SKILLS

Basic skills: Listening, speaking, mathematics, reading

Thinking: Decision making, problem solving, reasoning

COMPETENCIES

Resources: Time, materials and facilities

Information: Evaluates, organizes and maintains information; interprets and communicates information

Activity

Meet customers when they arrive and record relevant information as directed by the supervisor.

FOUNDATION SKILLS

Basic skills: Listening, speaking, writing

Thinking: Decision making, reasoning

COMPETENCIES

Information: Acquires and evaluates new information, interprets and communicates information

Interpersonal: Participates as team member, serves clients

Activity

Become proficient in the use of office data entry, using software such as Lotus 1-2-3 and Microsoft Excel.

FOUNDATION SKILLS

Basic skills: Reading, writing

Thinking: Problem solving, decision making, creative thinking

COMPETENCIES

Information: Acquires, evaluates, interprets, and communicates information; uses computers to process information

Systems: Understands systems, improves or designs systems

Activity

Demonstrate responsibility, self-esteem, and self-management required as a team member.

FOUNDATION SKILLS

Basic skills: Listening, speaking

Personal qualities: Self-esteem, responsibility, sociability, self-management

COMPETENCIES

Interpersonal: Participate as team member

Activity

As a medical intern, conduct procedures such as taking blood pressure, temperature, etc.

FOUNDATION SKILLS

Basic skills: Listening, speaking, reading

Thinking: Decision making, problem solving, reasoning

COMPETENCIES

Resources: Materials and facilities, serves clients

Information: Acquires, evaluates, interprets, and communicates information

Systems: Understands systems

Technology: Selects and applies technology

GENERAL INFORMATION

The following guidelines may help you understand the importance of professionalism, social manners, and behavior in the workplace.

Dress

Your first impression is always a lasting one. Your initial contact with the employer will most likely be the interview. For this important occasion, dress neatly with coat and tie, slacks, dress, or business suit. Minimum attire is suitable school clothes that are clean and neat. Above all, be clean and tidy. Shower, pull your hair back away from your face, and, if appropriate, wear small amounts of makeup and jewelry.

At the work site, dress codes may vary. Check with the business or agency for appropriate work dress for the rest of the experience.

AVOID

- T-shirts, torn or dirty clothes
- Excessive jewelry or piercings
- Shorts, tank tops, hats, or sweat pants

Behavior

Today's businesses are looking for young people with "good attitudes." What does that mean? It means employers are looking for people who display an optimistic view of life, who get things done, who promote good feelings, and who don't easily give up. When confronted with difficult situations, they are persistent, confident, and satisfied with their own capabilities. Today's jobs require a positive attitude.

Employers also look for good listeners. Good listening involves making eye contact, asking appropriate questions, and avoiding interrupting a speaker.

The ability to get along with others and display appropriate social behavior for the workplace is vital. The ability to adjust to new people around you, young and old, is an important skill. Getting along with others includes having a good sense of humor, showing an interest in others' work, listening, sharing, and teamwork.

AVOID

- Talking about personal issues (boyfriend/girlfriend, home, etc.) to others in the workplace
- Excessive talking, which will limit your productivity and that of coworkers.
- Complaining about school, home, or other people.
- Being late to work!
- Telling jokes. In addition, be culturally aware of others' feelings

Safety

Personal and environmental safety is very important for your work experience. Safety issues should be discussed at your business orientation. If they are not, ask questions such as:

> Where are the fire and emergency exits?
>
> Where are the restrooms located?
>
> Does my job require tools or machinery? If so, what kind?
>
> Do I need to wear protective equipment (hearing protection, glasses, gloves, etc.)?

Report any "uncomfortable" feelings or situations to the school site supervisor immediately. Remember, business employees should behave in a professional manner and respect your rights as a student.

AVOID

- Using equipment or tools if you are unsure about safety.
- Being alone in an enclosed area with another employee for long periods.
- Engaging in personal conversations.

Attendance

You are expected to arrive promptly for both school and work, including business meetings. Expect to arrive 10–15 minutes early to make sure you are not late.

Unexcused absences may require you to repeat the class or experience, and may result in termination from the activity. This also holds true for excessive excused absences. Your program coordinator will probably handle such issues on an individual basis.

You must follow the school procedures for absences the same way you do for all classes. Call the employer early in the morning if you must miss work for any reason.

AVOID

- Making unfounded excuses for being late or absent.
- Making excessive appointments during work hours.

Transportation

You will be required to arrange your own transportation to job interviews and work sites. Check the school guidelines for procedures regarding off-campus passes, risk management, and other pertinent information.

AVOID

- Planning rides to the work site with unreliable friends.
- Having friends wait for you at the business site.

Program

chapter 2

USING YOUR WORK-BASED LEARNING NOTEBOOK

Use the following guidelines as you proceed through the work-based learning program. This step-by-step procedure will help you complete all requirements. Check the appropriate boxes upon completion.

STEP 1: Before placement on a job site

❑ Meet with your teacher-coordinator or project director.

❑ Fulfill the readiness training requirement.

❑ Discuss and write an individual work-based learning plan.

❑ Review the notebook procedures and requirements specific to your program.

STEP 2: Placement

❑ Sign the work-based learning contract.

❑ Complete the application process.

❑ Tour the business facility.

❑ Complete site orientation.

❑ Complete training agreements.

❑ Complete job training.

❑ Complete the weekly tasks in the journal.

STEP 3: Final Tasks

❑ Complete midterm evaluations.

❑ Complete self and performance evaluations.

❑ Complete final project or presentation.

❑ Turn in journal to teacher/coordinator.

❑ Complete career pathway experience form for portfolio.

PROGRAM PROCEDURES AND REQUIREMENTS

Your work-based learning program will include experiences that are categorized as internships, mentorships, structured work experiences, or community service learning. Community sites are selected based upon the business or organization's interest, availability, and commitment to planning and participating in the program. You will be matched with a site based on your individual interest, readiness skill levels, availability, and commitment to participate.

Prerequisite: Student Readiness

Before you begin a community experience you must show that you are ready for placement. This means you must demonstrate your knowledge and understanding of appropriate work site manners, behaviors, and expectations. You can achieve this through classroom instruction, personal references, or previous work experience evaluations.

Program

School Orientations

All students will receive an overview of the work-based program, its purposes, goals, and requirements through class or individualized instruction. You will receive a personal notebook/journal and a review of its contents and will work together with the school coordinator to select an appropriate work-based learning site. This includes a review of business goals and objectives, long-range planning, philosophy, and management styles. Participation in the program will always require a signed contract.

Application Process

When you are matched to a community site, you will fill out a business application and prepare a written resume, which you will give to the employer at the interview. Interviews will always be required and held at the community site at a time agreed to by the school, the student, and the business. If your application is accepted, a work schedule that meets the needs of all parties will be developed.

Site Orientations

After being accepted by the community site, you will be given an orientation to the facility. This will occur on the first day of the learning experience. Orientations will include a general tour of the facility including confidential areas, restrooms and lunch areas, and workstations; an introduction to appropriate management, supervisors and clerical staff; and information about emergency and safety procedures.

Training Agreements

Within the first week of working, the employer/agency, student, and school coordinator are required to complete a formal training agreement. The agreement must include specific learning objectives relating to essential workplace skills that are identified by employers. Your individual needs as a student will also be included as part of the plan.

Job Training

Job training may be an ongoing process as you perform assigned tasks, or it may be limited to a specified time or number of days, depending on the business' requirements. Training may include a preplanning session, a review of student skills and abilities, an explanation of the specific work tasks, information about safety procedures, audio or video instruction or demonstration of the tasks, and follow-up procedures and evaluations.

Supervision

You will be matched to a direct supervisor who may or may not be the same person who performs your training sessions. In some cases you may have more than one supervisor. A business representative will facilitate communication and act as the liaison between the school and employer.

Evaluations

Each student will usually receive a midterm and a final evaluation of the work experience. Employers will rate and comment on the specific goals and objectives on your training agreement, behavior, work habits, and attitudes. You will also be evaluated on a project and class presentation if the coordinator requires one.

Journal

Each student will be issued a student notebook/journal for use during the experience. You are usually required to complete all the assignments in the journal as stated by the teacher/coordinator.

Student Project and Presentation

The teacher/coordinator may require each student to choose a problem, specific project, or summary related to the experience in the community. At the conclusion of the experience you may be asked to give a formal presentation to the class. The presentation guidelines will be included in your notebook.

My Work-Based Learning Plan

Name: _____ Date: _____

Interests: _____
_____
_____
_____
_____

Personal qualities: _____
_____
_____
_____
_____

Skills and abilities: _____
_____
_____
_____
_____

Short-term goals: _____
_____
_____
_____
_____

Long-term goals: _____
_____
_____
_____
_____

Work-Based Learning Plan

Previous work experiences:

_____

_____

_____

_____

_____

_____

References:

_____

_____

_____

_____

_____

My Work-Based Learning Contract

THE STUDENT LEARNER AGREES TO THE FOLLOWING RESPONSIBILITIES:

❏ Conform to the rules and regulations of the work-based learning program.

❏ Complete required program assignments.

❏ Keep regular attendance both at school and at the work site.

❏ Show honesty, punctuality, and a cooperative attitude, and wear proper attire.

❏ Consult the employer and school staff regarding concerns or problems.

❏ Conform to regulations at the work site and maintain confidentiality.

❏ Arrange transportation to and from the work site.

❏ Report all job-related accidents or illnesses immediately.

I agree to comply with all the regulations set forth by this program and the company to which I am assigned. I agree to maintain my citizenship responsibilities both in and out of school. Failure to comply with these rules may result in my removal from the program.

Student Signature: _____ **Date:** _____

Teacher Coordinator/Director: _____

The Business I Work For

Name of Business: _____

Location: _____

Number of Employees: _____

TYPE OF BUSINESS:

❏ Retail   ❏ Natural resources

❏ Business   ❏ Human services

❏ Health services   ❏ Industrial and engineering

❏ Arts and communication

Products and/or services: _____

_____

_____

Management style and organization: _____

_____

_____

WORKING CONDITIONS:

❏ Indoors   ❏ Noisy

❏ Outdoors   ❏ Travel required

❏ Heavy equipment   ❏ Friendly/relaxed

❏ Office atmosphere   ❏ Rigid/anxious

❏ Tools and machinery   ❏ Safe

❏ Quiet

Social activities: _____

_____

Rules and regulations: _____

_____

_____

Program Directory

Name: _____   School: _____

Program coordinator: _____   Phone: _____

E-mail: _____   Fax: _____

Work site program coordinator: _____   Phone: _____

E-mail: _____   Fax: _____

DIRECT WORK SUPERVISORS:

Name: _____

Department: _____   Phone: _____

E-mail: _____   Fax: _____

Name: _____

Department: _____   Phone: _____

E-mail: _____   Fax: _____

Name: _____

Department: _____   Phone: _____

E-mail: _____   Fax: _____

Name: _____

Department: _____   Phone _____

E-mail: _____   Fax: _____

Additional site information: _____

_____

_____

_____

_____

_____

_____

_____

Work-Based Learning Waiver Form

Name: _____

Student #: _____

School/class: _____

Semester: _____

Program coordinator: _____

Parent(s): _____

Address: _____

Phone: _____

E-mail: _____

The above-named student agrees to complete readiness training for community work-based learning. This includes instruction and demonstration of competency in personal grooming and manners, professionalism, work ethics, communication, and positive work habits and attitudes. This waiver form is a requirement for every student who is placed at a business site as part of the overall work-based learning system. By completing specific training or demonstrating competence, the student agrees to the code of conduct and confidentiality required by the program.

I understand that the program will not be responsible for my actions if I fail to follow the required training standards set by the program. I agree to indemnify and hold the program harmless with respect to any claims that may result from my behavior.

Student Signature: _____ Date: _____

Parent/Guardian Signature: _____ Date: _____

Journal

3

chapter

USING YOUR PERSONAL JOURNAL

The personal journal is designed for your use during your work-based experience. It will serve as a valuable record of your activities and provide information about you as a worker.

The journal has several important functions. First, it serves as a reminder of the program's goals and requirements. Second, you can use it to review important concepts and issues from the readiness activities you completed prior to the experience. Third, the journal provides an opportunity for you to identify specific skills and write about issues and concerns. Finally, it provides a record of the experience that you can add to your school portfolio.

REQUIREMENTS AND REMINDERS

1. Identify at least one SCANS competency or skill each week and write a paragraph about how you accomplished or performed the skill.

2. At the end of each week complete the weekly Commentary section.

3. Keep records of important dates and meetings in the Reflection pages. Also write thoughts and feelings in this section.

4. Remember, program coordinators, teachers, or work site supervisors may look at your journal during the week.

Journal Entry Example

Week 1: _____   Date: 1/22/2001

SCANS SKILL OR COMPETENCY IDENTIFIED: (See examples in Chapter 1)

I used the foundation skills of problem solving and decision making in my new job.

HOW ACCOMPLISHED:

This week I worked in the customer service department. I had to make decisions about returned items that customers brought in for refunds, and where to send them for assistance if a problem occurred. I consulted with other employees and learned from watching their responses. I also had to answer the phone and make decisions about transferring people to other departments.

COMMENTARY:

Describe your personal feelings and frame of mind during your first week on the job.

At first I was a little nervous when I was placed in the customer service department. I thought people would be angry and rude when they brought in their products. Actually, most all the customers were nice and we discussed their needs in a responsible manner. Most everyone was polite and went away feeling like they received satisfactory help. I worked alongside one other employee who made me feel relaxed and calm.

   My most difficult situation was when a person brought in damaged merchandise. I was required to send him to the floor manager for assistance. Everything worked out fine. Answering the phone was not a problem. I felt confident and assured that I transferred people to the correct departments for assistance.

Journal Entry 1

Week 1: _____ **Date:** _____

SCANS SKILL OR COMPETENCY IDENTIFIED: (See examples in Chapter 1)

_____

_____

_____

HOW ACCOMPLISHED:

_____

_____

_____

_____

_____

_____

_____

_____

COMMENTARY:

Describe the application process and interview. What were the most difficult questions and how did you answer?
Rate your overall performance.

_____

_____

_____

_____

_____

_____

_____

_____

_____

_____

_____

Journal Entry 2

Week 2: _____   Date: _____

SCANS SKILL OR COMPETENCY IDENTIFIED: (See examples in Chapter 1)

_____

_____

_____

HOW ACCOMPLISHED:

_____

_____

_____

_____

_____

_____

_____

COMMENTARY:

Describe the student orientation and training process at your community work site. Was it adequate and complete?

_____

_____

_____

_____

_____

_____

_____

_____

_____

_____

_____

Journal Entry 2

Journal Entry 3

Week 3: _____ **Date:** _____

SCANS SKILL OR COMPETENCY IDENTIFIED: (See examples in Chapter 1)

_____

_____

_____

HOW ACCOMPLISHED:

_____

_____

_____

_____

_____

_____

_____

COMMENTARY:

Do you feel comfortable at your work site? How are you treated? Describe the work environment.

_____

_____

_____

_____

_____

_____

_____

_____

_____

_____

_____

Journal Entry 3

Journal Entry 4

Week 4: _____   **Date:** _____

SCANS SKILL OR COMPETENCY IDENTIFIED: (See examples in Chapter 1)

_____

_____

_____

HOW ACCOMPLISHED:

_____

_____

_____

_____

_____

_____

_____

COMMENTARY:

Describe your specific tasks at work. What equipment do you use? Do you work alone or in a group? Do you perform a daily routine or do tasks change each time you work?

_____

_____

_____

_____

_____

_____

_____

_____

_____

_____

_____

Week 5: _____   Date: _____

SCANS SKILL OR COMPETENCY IDENTIFIED: (See examples in Chapter 1)

_____

_____

_____

HOW ACCOMPLISHED:

_____

_____

_____

_____

_____

_____

_____

COMMENTARY:

What is your relationship with management, supervisors, and co-workers? Are you receiving the assistance you need to be successful?

_____

_____

_____

_____

_____

_____

_____

_____

_____

_____

WORKSHEET

Journal Entry 6

Week 6: _____ **Date:** _____

SCANS SKILL OR COMPETENCY IDENTIFIED: (See examples in Chapter 1)

_____

_____

_____

HOW ACCOMPLISHED:

_____

_____

_____

_____

_____

_____

_____

COMMENTARY:

Describe your community work site. Is it safe? Does anyone need protective equipment? Where are potential hazards located?

_____

_____

_____

_____

_____

_____

_____

_____

_____

_____

_____

Week 7: _____ **Date:** _____

SCANS SKILL OR COMPETENCY IDENTIFIED: (See examples in Chapter 1)

_____

_____

_____

HOW ACCOMPLISHED:

_____

_____

_____

_____

_____

_____

_____

COMMENTARY:

What are the ethical standards for this work site? How does your business or agency exhibit appropriate work ethics?

_____

_____

_____

_____

_____

_____

_____

_____

_____

_____

Journal Entry 8

Week 8: _____   **Date:** _____

SCANS SKILL OR COMPETENCY IDENTIFIED: (See examples in Chapter 1)

_____

_____

_____

HOW ACCOMPLISHED:

_____

_____

_____

_____

_____

_____

_____

COMMENTARY:

Discuss some of the business rules and policies you feel are important not only for work, but for daily life.

_____

_____

_____

_____

_____

_____

_____

_____

_____

_____

_____

_____

Journal Entry 8

Journal Entry 9

Week 9: _____ **Date:** _____

SCANS SKILL OR COMPETENCY IDENTIFIED: (See examples in Chapter 1)

_____

_____

_____

HOW ACCOMPLISHED:

_____

_____

_____

_____

_____

_____

_____

COMMENTARY:

Cooperation and teamwork are important elements of any organization. How does your work site display cooperation and teamwork? How are you involved in these activities?

_____

_____

_____

_____

_____

_____

_____

_____

_____

_____

_____

Journal Entry 9

Journal Entry 10

WORKSHEET

Week 10: _____ Date: _____

SCANS SKILL OR COMPETENCY IDENTIFIED: (See examples in Chapter 1)

_____

_____

_____

HOW ACCOMPLISHED:

_____

_____

_____

_____

_____

_____

_____

COMMENTARY:

How has this work experience changed your views of the community, your personal goals, and school?

_____

_____

_____

_____

_____

_____

_____

_____

_____

_____

_____

Reflections

Identify and describe your feelings, thoughts, and ideas. Record meeting dates or general business news. Use this information for presentation, evaluation, or other uses.

Final Presentation

PRESENTATION GUIDELINES

At the conclusion of the work experience, each student should give a minimum 10-minute oral presentation. You may choose to present an overview of the learning experience, or to describe a problem that you helped solve at the business site. Presentations can be given to a class, a selected group of peers, or program staff members.

Include visuals in your presentation. Visuals may include a Power Point presentation, charts and graphs, and written summaries or handouts for the audience.

Submit an outline of your presentation to the supervising teacher-coordinator for review, one week before the scheduled presentation.

Presenting an Overview

If you choose to give an overview of your experience, use the following format for the presentation.

1. Identify the type of business, size, employees, demographics.

2. Review the application and interview process.

3. Discuss the student orientation and training.

4. Review the tasks you performed.

5. Discuss any barriers or problems you encountered.

6. Describe what you learned from the experience.

Presenting a Problem

Students who choose to tackle a problem should use the following problem-solving guidelines.

1. Identify the problem.

2. Gather information.

3. Use available resources.

4. Analyze the data you have gathered.

5. Prepare an action plan.

6. Identify the steps for making it work.

7. Put the plan into action.

8. Evaluate the results.

9. Make recommendations or changes as necessary.

At the conclusion of the presentation you should be prepared to answer questions from the audience and supervising teacher.

The following pages will guide you through taking notes and planning your presentation as you progress in your work experience.

Presentation Evaluation WORKSHEET

Name: _____ Date: _____

Topic or Problem: _____

	Excellent		Average		Poor
CONTENT					
Clear and focused objectives and purpose	5	4	3	2	1
Support for findings; details	5	4	3	2	1
Reasonable and clearly stated arguments and recommendations	5	4	3	2	1
Content adapted to the audience and purpose	5	4	3	2	1
ORGANIZATION					
Easy-to-follow style	5	4	3	2	1
Effective introduction	5	4	3	2	1
Structure of details and facts	5	4	3	2	1
Summary and conclusions	5	4	3	2	1
LANGUAGE					
Appropriate business language	5	4	3	2	1
Clarity of message	5	4	3	2	1
Grammar and usage	5	4	3	2	1
Explanation of technical language	5	4	3	2	1
DELIVERY					
Control and poise	5	4	3	2	1
Self-confidence and voice projection	5	4	3	2	1
Pronunciation, tone, and inflection	5	4	3	2	1
Visual cues and prompts	5	4	3	2	1

TOTAL _____

Evaluations

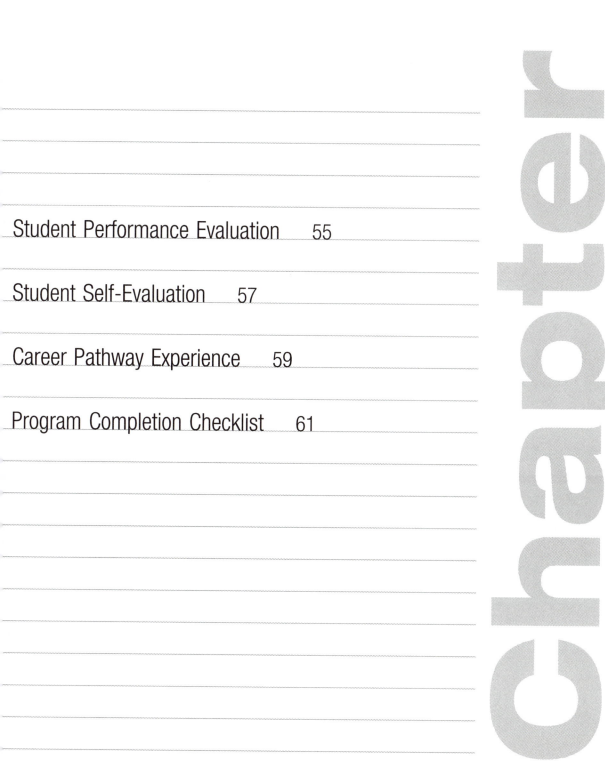

5

chapter

Student Performance Evaluation

(To be completed by school or work site supervisor)

Student Name: _____

Evaluator Name: _____

School: _____ **Date:** _____

Directions: For each statement, circle the response that best describes the student's performance. Please comment if appropriate.

1. The student shows enthusiasm and interest in the program.

   STRONGLY AGREE   AGREE   DISAGREE   STRONGLY DISAGREE

   Comments: _____

   _____

2. The student participated in all the program activities.

   STRONGLY AGREE   AGREE   DISAGREE   STRONGLY DISAGREE

   Comments: _____

   _____

3. The student demonstrated appropriate attendance and punctuality.

   STRONGLY AGREE   AGREE   DISAGREE   STRONGLY DISAGREE

   Comments: _____

   _____

4. The student demonstrated appropriate communication skills, including ability to listen, ask appropriate questions, and use appropriate language.

   STRONGLY AGREE   AGREE   DISAGREE   STRONGLY DISAGREE

   Comments: _____

   _____

5. The student demonstrated the ability to adapt to changes in the program and work.

   STRONGLY AGREE   AGREE   DISAGREE   STRONGLY DISAGREE

   Comments: _____

   _____

6. The student demonstrated appropriate dress and appearance.

STRONGLY AGREE   AGREE   DISAGREE   STRONGLY DISAGREE

Comments: _____
_____

7. The student's behavior and manners were appropriate for the experience.

STRONGLY AGREE   AGREE   DISAGREE   STRONGLY DISAGREE

Comments : _____
_____

8. The student notified appropriate parties if ill or for emergencies.

STRONGLY AGREE   AGREE   DISAGREE   STRONGLY DISAGREE

Comments : _____
_____

9. The student practiced safety in all activities.

STRONGLY AGREE   AGREE   DISAGREE   STRONGLY DISAGREE

Comments : _____
_____

10. The student followed directions and program requirements.

STRONGLY AGREE   AGREE   DISAGREE   STRONGLY DISAGREE

Comments : _____
_____

11. The student completed assigned tasks on time without reminders.

STRONGLY AGREE   AGREE   DISAGREE   STRONGLY DISAGREE

Comments : _____
_____

12. The student demonstrated teamwork by getting along with others, working cooperatively in groups, and participating in group activities.

STRONGLY AGREE   AGREE   DISAGREE   STRONGLY DISAGREE

Comments : _____
_____

Student Self Evaluation

Name: _____

School/Program: _____ Date: _____

Directions: For each statement, circle the response that best describes your participation in the program.

1. I had adequate information and introductions to begin the program.

   STRONGLY AGREE   AGREE   DISAGREE   STRONGLY DISAGREE

   Comments: _____

   _____

   _____

2. I felt supported by my school-based supervisor.

   STRONGLY AGREE   AGREE   DISAGREE   STRONGLY DISAGREE

   Comments: _____

   _____

   _____

3. My work site supervisors were helpful and showed an interest in my progress and the program.

   STRONGLY AGREE   AGREE   DISAGREE   STRONGLY DISAGREE

   Comments: _____

   _____

   _____

4. The program has helped my future career awareness and goals.

   STRONGLY AGREE   AGREE   DISAGREE   STRONGLY DISAGREE

   Comments: _____

   _____

   _____

5. My work site provided me with a variety of learning opportunities.

   STRONGLY AGREE   AGREE   DISAGREE   STRONGLY DISAGREE

   Comments: _____

   _____

   _____

6. The program helped me understand how my school work and activities are directly related to the workplace.

STRONGLY AGREE   AGREE   DISAGREE   STRONGLY DISAGREE

Comments: _____

_____

_____

7. I completed tasks and followed directions to the best of my ability.

STRONGLY AGREE   AGREE   DISAGREE   STRONGLY DISAGREE

Comments: _____

_____

_____

8. I would recommend this program to another student.

STRONGLY AGREE   AGREE   DISAGREE   STRONGLY DISAGREE

Comments: _____

_____

_____

List the five activities you enjoyed most during the program.

1. _____

_____

2. _____

_____

3. _____

_____

4. _____

_____

5. _____

_____

Career Pathway Experience

(To be added to the student portfolio)

Name: _____

Address: _____

_____

Phone: _____ **E-mail:** _____

Student ID No.: _____ **School/Program:** _____

WORK-BASED LEARNING OPPORTUNITY

❑ Visitation/field trip   ❑ Internship

❑ Shadow   ❑ Structured work experience

❑ Mentorship   ❑ Service learning

Site: _____

Supervisor: _____

Dates Worked: *from* _____ *to* _____

Hours/days worked: _____

Year in school: _____ **Quarter/semester:** _____

Activities completed:

❑ Readiness training   ❑ On-site training

❑ Resume   ❑ Evaluations

❑ Application   ❑ Journal

❑ Interview   ❑ Project or classroom presentation

❑ Orientation

❑ Attached evaluation or recommendation letter to portfolio

Student Performance Evaluation

Name: _____ Date: _____

Program: _____

Teacher/coordinator program director completes this checklist at the conclusion of the experience. Students should complete all areas to receive a grade and/or credit for the experience.

	Date Completed	Coordinator Signature
Attendance	_____	_____
Notebook/Journal completed *(including weekly journal entries)*	_____	_____
Presentation	_____	_____
Evaluations	_____	_____
Graduation date *(if applicable)*	_____	_____

Notes

Notes

Notes

Notes

Notes

Notes

Notes

Notes